Sticker

Activity Books

Time

Note to parents and teachers

This sticker book is specially designed to help young children learn about time. A wide range of puzzles covers basic time concepts and introduces the first stages of learning to tell the time. As you work through the book with your child, you will find that the puzzles gradually become more difficult – from finding things to use during the day and night, to matching times shown on clocks and watches. Adult help will ensure that children get the most from these books, and children under three should definitely be supervised when using the stickers.

The wide variety of colourful pictures provides lots of talking points and will help to capture and hold your child's attention. Each picture is labelled, linking the image to the written word – one of the first steps in learning to read.

The stickers are clearly grouped by page number so you can help your child to find the right stickers for each activity. But children can also have fun finding other ways to play with the stickers by decorating notebooks or making sticker pictures or posters.

 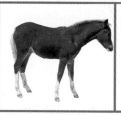    

Daytime

Can you find things that you would use during the day?

Night-time

Can you find things that you would use at night?

Morning

Can you find breakfast things for Bobby to eat and drink?

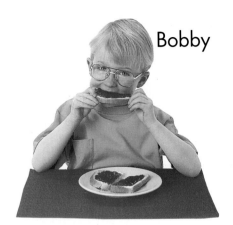

Bobby

Afternoon

Can you find things for Jane to use at school?

Jane

Evening

Can you find things for Joe to use at bathtime?

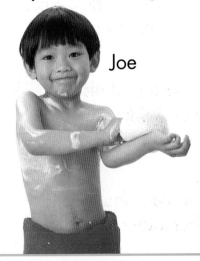

Joe

In a week

Can you use stickers to show what Kate did in a week?

Monday	**Friday**
Tuesday	**Saturday**
Wednesday	**Sunday**
Thursday	

Kate went to the beach on both days of the weekend.

On Tuesday, Kate went to art class.

Kate played a ball game on Wednesday.

Kate went to a birthday party on Friday.

Kate's music lesson was on Monday.

Kate went shopping on Thursday afternoon.

Through the year
Can you find things that go with each season?

Spring

Summer

Autumn

Winter

Stickers
Page 3

Page 6

Page 4

Page 5

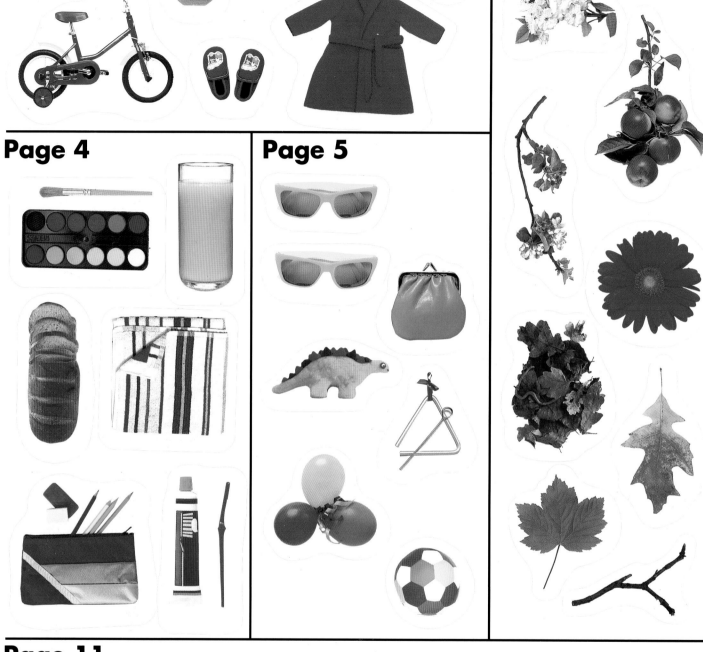

Page 11

Page 12

Page 13

 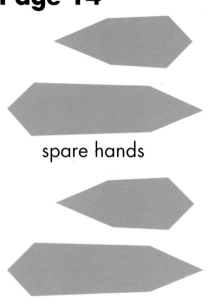

Page 14

spare hands

Page 15

| quarter past seven | quarter past ten |

| half past five | seven o'clock |

Growing things

As time passes, things grow and change. Can you find the missing pictures?

Human

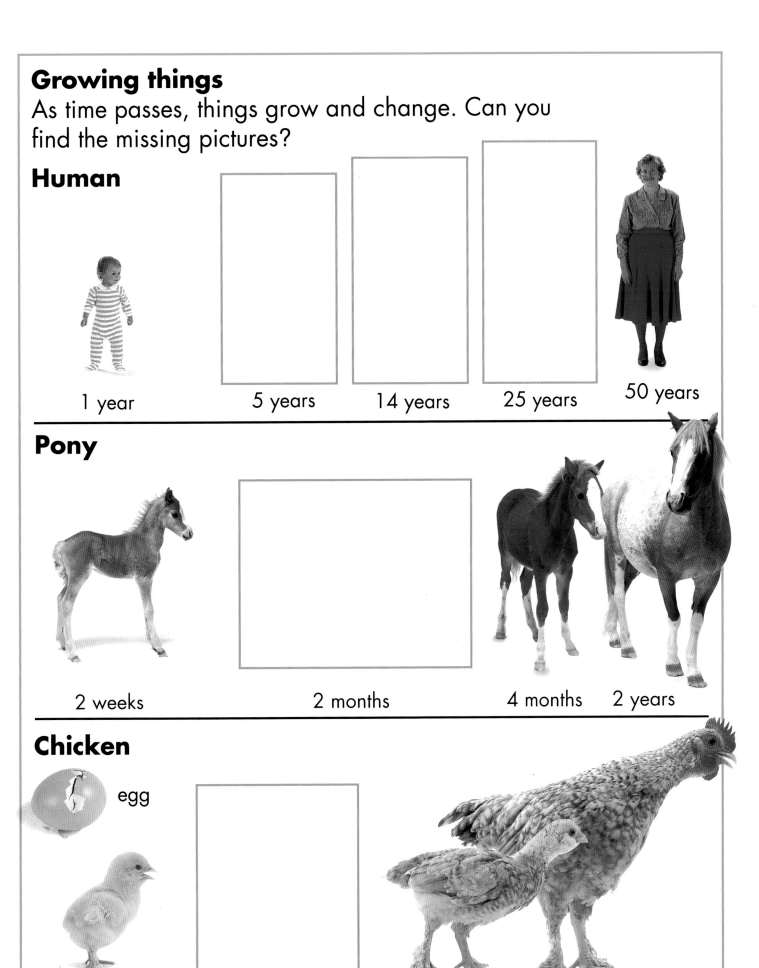

1 year

5 years

14 years

25 years

50 years

Pony

2 weeks

2 months

4 months   2 years

Chicken

egg

3 days

2 weeks

4 weeks   8 weeks

On the hour

Can you find clocks that match the times on these clocks?

six o'clock

two o'clock

nine o'clock

eleven o'clock

twelve o'clock

Digital times

Can you find digital clocks and watches to match these times?

five o'clock 5:00

eight o'clock 8:00

four o'clock 4:00

one o'clock 1:00

ten o'clock 10:00

three o'clock 3:00

Moving hands

Can you use the sticker hands to show the same times as on these clocks and watches? *

quarter past seven

half past seven

quarter to eleven

quarter to three

quarter past four

half past two

*First place the sticker hands on some card and cut round each one.

Mix and match

Can you find stickers to match the times shown on this page?

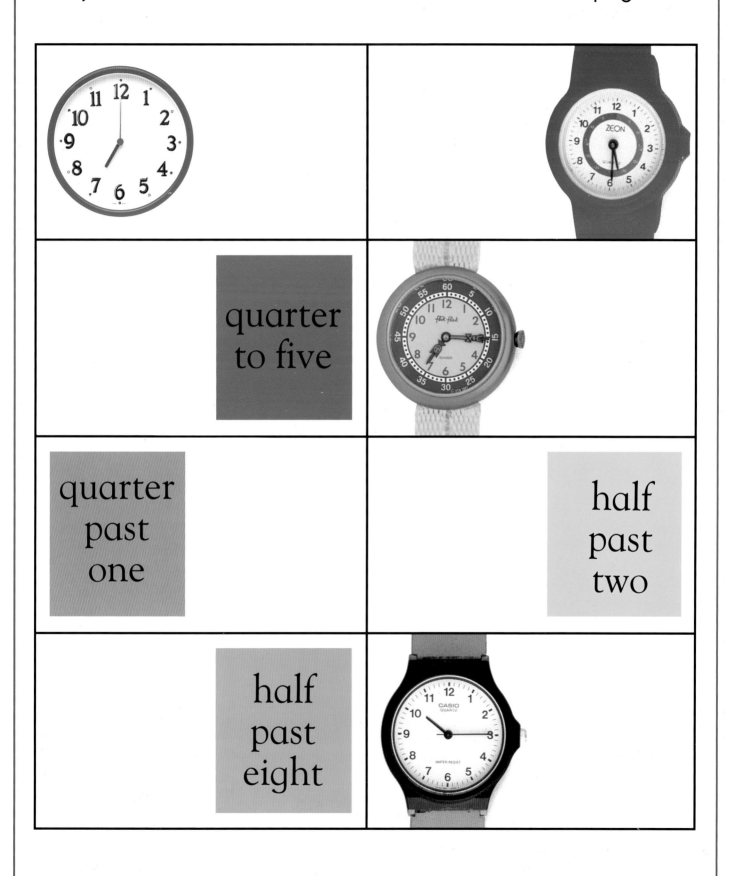

quarter
to five

quarter
past
one

half
past
two

half
past
eight

DK

**LONDON, NEW YORK, MELBOURNE,
MUNICH AND DELHI**

Assistant Editor Finbar Hawkins
Senior Editor Sheila Hanly
Art Editor Sharon Peters
Production Susannah Straughan

Artwork
Julie Carpenter
Graham Philpot

Published in Great Britain by
Dorling Kindersley Limited,
80 Strand, London WC2R 0RL

4 6 8 10 9 7 5 3

Visit us on the World Wide Web at http://www.dk.com

A CIP catalogue record for this book
is available from the British Library.

ISBN 1405312556

Colour reproduction by Colourscan, Singapore
Printed and bound in China

Unsuitable for children under three
because of small parts